OTTO
The Otter
A BIG SURPRISE

Written & Illustrated by

Linda Hansen

Written & Illustrated by Linda Hansen.
Graphic design by Praise Saflor

Printed in the United States

Publisher's Cataloging-in-Publication Data

Names: Hansen, Linda, author.
Title: Otto the otter : a big surprise / Linda Hansen.
Description: Largo, FL: Linda Hansen, 2022. | Summary: A North American river otter raises her family.
Identifiers: LCCN: 2021918055 | ISBN: 978-1-7378308-1-8 (hardcover) |
978-1-7378308-2-5 (paperback) | 978-1-7378308-0-1 (ebook)
Subjects: LCSH North American river otter--Juvenile literature. | Otters--Juvenile literature. |
CYAC North American river otter. | Otters. | BISAC JUVENILE NONFICTION / Animals /
Mammals | JUVENILE NONFICTION / Animals / Marine Life
Classification: LCC QL737.C25 .H36 2022 | DDC 599.74/447--dc23

This book is dedicated to

—Roni, my dear friend and neighbor, without whose urging
Otto the Otter, A Big Surprise would never have been written...

—My watercolor teachers, whose inspiration and guidance
helped me develop the skills I never knew I had.

—My husband, Gary, for supporting me in all my endeavors.

Otto the otter has been visiting this small pond for a long time.

The people who live in the grey house near the pond gave him his name. It is always a wonderful **surprise** when they see him.

Otto doesn't come *every day*, but he does come often - to swim, play and eat. Otto stays at the pond for a few hours and then travels from the pond, through a creek, to another pond nearby. Otters travel in a six-mile area and the people's pond is just one of the places he visits.

Otto is a North American River Otter and he lives in fresh water. River Otters are different from Sea Otters, who live in the salty water of the Pacific Ocean. Otters sleep near water in a variety of places on land, both above ground and in underground dens.

Otto leaves the pond at night. The people in the grey house don't know where he goes. Sometimes they see him leave as he squeezes through the fence on the other side of the pond.

The people worry about Otto if they don't see him for a long time. Once, he stayed away all winter and finally showed up again in the spring— with a very BIG SURPRISE...

Otto turned out to NOT be Otto!

Otto is a girl!

How did the people realize that Otto is a girl?
Otto came to the pond with two babies!
The people changed the otter's name to Opal.

Otter babies are called pups. Before they are born, their mother creates a quiet den where they will be born and kept safe. The pups spend their first month there. They can't see because their eyes are not open yet, but their mom watches over them.

As the pups grow, the small pond near the grey house provides a safe place for them. The first few weeks that Opal brought them to the pond, they stayed all day. Their mom always keeps them close and looks after them.

The people in the grey house never get tired of watching them.

When the pups were about two months old, Opal started to teach them to swim. The pups were not born knowing how to swim. Their mom also taught them how to look for food under the water.

Otters eat fish, frogs, crayfish, turtles, and insects. They have long whiskers, which help them find their food in dark or cloudy water. They also have special eyelids, which allow them to keep their eyes open to see while swimming under the water.

Otters can close their ears and noses, which allows them to swim under water for almost eight minutes.

Sometimes the otters disappear under the water, but the people can tell where they are by the bubbles that rise to the surface.

The pups often leave the pond to play on the grass, clean themselves and nurse from Opal. Mother otters continue to cuddle and nurse their pups for 14 weeks.

As the pups continue to grow, they leave Opal's side and swim around the pond to explore and play on their own. Opal watches them very closely and squeaks loudly to show them her displeasure when they get too far away.

There are two wooden rafts floating in the small pond. The people who live in the grey house call them *turtle islands*. During the heat of the day, the turtles who live in the pond like to climb onto the rafts and enjoy the warmth of the sun.

The pups love to play on the *turtle islands* too.
When the pups are on the raft, the turtles leave to
find another place to enjoy their time in the sun.

The people in the grey house love to watch the otters swim. Otters have long, flat, wide tails that they use just like a rudder on a boat. Their tail helps them steer, and also helps them swim fast.

Adult otters are very strong and can swim 6 to 7 miles per hour while in the water, and can run as fast as 15 miles per hour on land.

The people watch as time passes and the pups continue to grow. Opal moves them from the safety of the pond more often and takes them to other places.

Sometimes they are gone for several days. Now, when they do come, they no longer stay very long. Their lives have become busier as they travel from pond to pond.

The people in the grey house do not know how long or how often they will get to see Opal and her pups. Otter pups usually stay with their mother until they are a year old. The people hope they will get to see them for a long time and watch them grow.

If the people in the grey house are lucky, maybe Opal will show up with a new litter of pups one day.

This painting was done by Sophia, my neighbor, when she was 7 years old. Sophia often comes to paint with me.

Opal and her pups resting on the turtle island.

LINDA HANSEN

Linda Hansen loves combining art and nature. After retiring from her career as the Executive Director of a non-profit, she has finally found the time to follow her creative passions. She is currently working in watercolor and is both the author and illustrator of this creative children's book.

Linda grew up in St. Louis, Missouri and currently lives in Florida with her husband and two dogs—very close to the small pond where this true story takes place.

You can contact Linda at www.lindahansenauthor.com

www.facebook.com/lindahansenauthor

Visit our website and sign up to get updates,
information and be entered into a drawing for
a free gift featuring Opal and/or her pups.

www.lindahansenauthor.com

SCAN ME